ISBN-13:    978-1500648473

ISBN-10:    1500648477

rgurel@yahoo.com

# Table of contents

# Preface

This book is the first one in a series of books about arcade, video and computer games. As an enthusiastic game player, I decided to collect information about the games I played and liked. Actually it is a handpicked collection of articles from various sources (especially wikipedia.org). You can find the links to the original articles in the "References" section of each game.

All the copyrighted materials in this book belong to their respective owners.

24 April 2014

Rafet GUREL

# 1. PONG

Pong (marketed as PONG) is one of the earliest arcade video games. It is a tennis sports game

featuring simple two-dimensional graphics. While other arcade video games such as Computer Space came before it, Pong was one of the first video games to reach mainstream popularity. The aim is to defeat an opponent in a simulated table tennis game by earning a higher score. The game was originally manufactured by Atari Incorporated (Atari), who released it in 1972. Allan ALCORN created Pong as a training exercise assigned to him by Atari cofounder Nolan BUSHNELL. Bushnell based the idea on an electronic Ping-Pong game included in the Magnavox Odyssey, which later resulted in a lawsuit against Atari. Surprised by the quality of Alcorn's work, Bushnell and Dabney decided to manufacture the game.

Pong quickly became a success and is the first commercially successful video game, which led to the start of the video game industry. Soon after its release, several companies began producing games that copied Pong's gameplay, and eventually released new types of games. As a result, Atari encouraged its staff to produce more innovative games. The company released several sequels that built upon the original's gameplay by adding new features. During the 1975 Christmas season, Atari released a home version of Pong exclusively through Sears retail stores. It was also a commercial success and led to numerous copies. The game has been remade on numerous home and portable platforms following its release. Pong has been referenced and parodied in multiple television shows and video games, and has been a part of several video game and cultural exhibitions.

Atari engineer Allan ALCORN designed and built Pong as a training exercise.

## 1.1. Gameplay

Pong is a two-dimensional sports game that simulates table tennis. The player controls an in-game paddle by moving it vertically across the left side of the screen, and can compete against either a computer-controlled opponent or another player controlling a second paddle on the opposing side. Players use the paddles to hit a ball back and forth. The aim is for each player to reach eleven points before the opponent. Points are earned when one fails to return the ball to the other.

## 1.2. Development and history

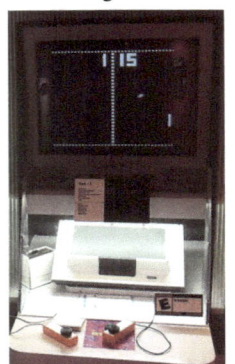

Magnavox Odyssey gaming console playing Pong.

Pong was the first game developed by Atari Inc., incorporated in June 1972 by Nolan BUSHNELL and Ted DABNEY. After producing Computer Space, Bushnell decided to form a company to produce more games by licensing ideas to other companies. The first contract was with Bally Manufacturing Corporation for a driving game. Soon after the founding, Bushnell hired Allan ALCORN because of his experience with electrical engineering and computer science. Bushnell and Dabney also had previously worked with him at Ampex. Prior to working at Atari, Alcorn had no experience with video games. To acclimate Alcorn to creating games, Bushnell gave him a project secretly meant to be a warm-up exercise. Bushnell told Alcorn that he had a contract with General Electric for a product, and asked Alcorn to create a simple game with one moving spot, two paddles, and digits for score keeping. In 2011, Bushnell stated that the game was inspired by previous versions of electronic tennis he had played before. Bushnell played a version on a PDP-1 computer in 1964 while attending college. However, Alcorn has claimed it was in direct response to Nolan's viewing of the Magnavox Odyssey's Tennis game. In May 1972, Bushnell had visited the Magnavox Profit Caravan in Burlingame, California where he played the Magnavox Odyssey demonstration, specifically the table tennis game. Though he thought the game lacked quality, seeing it, prompted Bushnell to assign the project to Alcorn.

Alcorn first examined Bushnell's schematics for Computer Space, but found them to be illegible. He went on to create his own designs based on his knowledge of transistor-transistor logic and Bushnell's game. Feeling the basic game was too boring, Alcorn added features to give the game more appeal. He divided the paddle into eight segments to change the ball's angle of return. For example, the center segments return the ball a 90° angle in relation to the paddle, while the outer segments return the ball at smaller angles. He also made the ball accelerate the longer it remained in play. Missing the ball reset the speed. Another feature was that the in-game paddles were unable to reach the top of screen. This was caused by a simple circuit that had an inherent defect. Instead of dedicating time to fixing the defect,

Alcorn decided it gave the game more difficulty and helped limit the time the game could be played. He

imagined two skilled players being able to play forever otherwise.

Three months into development, Bushnell told Alcorn he wanted the game to feature realistic sound effects and a roaring crowd. Dabney wanted the game to "boo" and "hiss" when a player lost a round. Alcorn had limited space available for the necessary electronics and was unaware of how to create such sounds with digital circuits. After inspecting the sync generator, he discovered that it could generate different tones and used those for the game's sound effects. To construct the prototype, Alcorn purchased a $75 Hitachi black and white television set from a local store, placed it into a 4 foot (1.2 m) wooden cabinet, and soldered the wires into boards to create the necessary circuitry. The prototype impressed Bushnell and Dabney so much that they felt it could be a profitable product and decided to test its marketability.

In August 1972, Bushnell and Alcorn installed the Pong prototype at a local bar, Andy Capp's Tavern. They selected the bar because of their good working relation with the bar's manager, Bill GATTIS. Atari supplied pinball machines to Gattis. Bushnell and Alcorn placed the prototype on one of the tables near the other entertainment machines: a jukebox, pinball machines and Computer Space. The game was well received the first night and its popularity continued to grow over the next one and a half weeks. Bushnell then went on a business trip to Chicago to demonstrate Pong to executives at Bally and

Midway Manufacturing. He intended to use Pong to fulfill his contract with Bally, rather than the

Al ALCORN with Pong at the opening event of Computer History Museum's Revolution exhibition.

driving game. A few days later, the prototype began exhibiting technical issues and Gattis contacted Alcorn to fix it. Upon inspecting the machine, Alcorn discovered that the problem was the coin mechanism was overflowing with quarters.

After hearing about the game's success, Bushnell decided there would be more profit for Atari to manufacture the game rather than license it, but the interest of Bally and Midway had already been piqued. Bushnell decided to inform each of the two groups that the other was uninterested (Bushnell told the Bally executives that the Midway executives did not want it and vice versa) to preserve the relationships for future dealings. Upon hearing Bushnell's comment, the two groups declined his offer. Bushnell had difficulty finding financial backing for Pong. Banks viewed it as a variant of pinball, which at the time the general public associated with the Mafia. Atari eventually obtained a line of credit from Wells Fargo that it used to expand its facilities to house an assembly line. The company announced "Pong" on 29 November 1972. Management sought assembly workers at the local unemployment office, but was unable to keep up with demand. The first arcade cabinets produced were assembled very slowly, about ten machines a day, many of which failed quality testing. Atari eventually streamlined the process and began producing the game in greater quantities. By 1973, they began shipping Pong to other countries with the aid of foreign partners.

Paddle of the Atari Pong arcade cabinet.

## 1.3. Home version

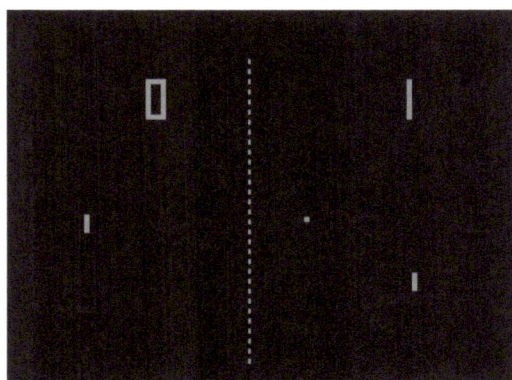

The two paddles return the ball back and forth. The score is kept by the numbers (0 and 1) at the top of the screen.

The success of Pong resulted in Bushnell pushing his employees to create new products. In 1974, Atari engineer Harold LEE proposed a home version of Pong that would connect to a television: Home Pong. The system began development under the codename Darlene, named after an attractive female employee at Atari. Alcorn worked with Lee to develop the designs and prototype, and based them on the same digital technology used in their arcade games. The two worked in shifts to save time and money. Lee worked on the design's logic during the day, while Alcorn debugged the designs in the evenings. After the designs were approved, fellow Atari engineer Bob BROWN assisted Alcorn and Lee in building a prototype. The prototype consisted of a device attached to a wooden pedestal containing over a hundred wires, which would eventually be replaced with a single chip designed by Alcorn and Lee. The chip had yet to be tested and built before the prototype was constructed. The chip was finished in the latter half of 1974, and was, at the time, the highest performing chip used in a consumer product.

Bushnell and Gene LIPKIN, Atari's vice president of sales, approached toy and electronic retailers to sell Home Pong, but were rejected. Retailers felt the product was too expensive and would not interest consumers. Atari contacted the Sears Sporting Goods department after noticing a Magnavox Odyssey advertisement in the sporting goods section of its catalog. Atari staff discussed the game with a representative, Tom QUINN, who expressed enthusiasm and offered the company an exclusive deal. Believing they could find more favorable terms elsewhere, Atari's executives declined and continued to pursue toy retailers. In January 1975, Atari staff set up a Home Pong booth at a toy trade fair in New York City, but was unsuccessful in soliciting orders.

While at the show, they met Quinn again, and a few days later, set up a meeting with him to obtain a sales order. In order to gain approval from the Sporting Goods department, Quinn suggested Atari demonstrate the game to executives in Chicago. Alcorn and Lipkin traveled to the Sears Tower and, despite a technical complication, obtained approval. Bushnell told Quinn he could produce 75,000 units in time for the Christmas season; however Quinn requested double the amount. Though Bushnell knew Atari lacked the capacity to manufacture 150,000 units, he agreed. Atari acquired a new factory through funding obtained by venture capitalist Don VALENTINE. Supervised by Jimm TUBB, the factory fulfilled the Sears order. The first units manufactured were branded with Sears' "Tele-Games" name. Atari later released a version under its own brand in 1976.

## 1.4. Lawsuit from Magnavox

The success of Pong attracted the attention of Ralph BAER, the inventor of the Magnavox Odyssey, and his employer, Sanders Associates. Sanders had an agreement with Magnavox to handle the Odyssey's sublicensing, which included dealing with infringement on its exclusive rights. However, Magnavox had not pursued legal action against Atari and numerous other companies that released Pong clones. Sanders continued to apply pressure, and in April 1974 Magnavox filed suit against Atari, Bally Midway, Allied Leisure and Chicago Dynamics. Magnavox argued that Atari had infringed on Baer's patents and his concept of electronic Ping-Pong based on detailed records Sanders kept of the Odyssey's design process dating back to 1966. Other documents included depositions from witnesses and a signed guest book that demonstrated Bushnell had played the Odyssey's table tennis game prior to releasing Pong. In response to claims that he saw the Odyssey, Bushnell later stated that, "The fact is that I absolutely did see the Odyssey game and I didn't think it was very clever".

After considering his options, Bushnell decided to settle with Magnavox out of court. Bushnell's lawyer felt they could win, however, he estimated legal costs of US$1.5 million, which would have exceeded Atari's funds. Magnavox offered Atari an agreement to become a licensee for US$0.7 million.

An upright cabinet of Pong signed by Pong creator Allan ALCORN.

Other companies producing "Pong clones" (Atari's competitors) would have to pay royalties. In addition, Magnavox would obtain the rights to Atari products developed over the next year. Magnavox continued to pursue legal action against the other companies, and proceedings began shortly after Atari's settlement in June 1976. The first case took place at the district court in Chicago, with Judge John GRADY presiding. To avoid Magnavox obtaining rights to its products, Atari decided to delay the release of its products for a year, and withheld information from Magnavox' attorneys during visits to Atari facilities.

Atari Video Pinball C-380. The second white model.

## 1.5. Impact and legacy

The Pong arcade games manufactured by Atari were a great success. The prototype was well received by Andy Capp's Tavern patrons. People came to the bar solely to play the game. Following its release, Pong consistently earned four times more revenue than other coin-operated machines. Bushnell estimated that the game earned US$35 - 40 per day, which he described as nothing he'd ever seen before in the coin-operated entertainment industry at the time. The game's earning power resulted in an increase in the number of orders Atari received.

Video pinball console.

This provided Atari with a steady source of income. The company sold the machines at three times the cost of production. By 1973, the company had filled 2,500 orders, and at the end of 1974, sold more than 8,000 units. The arcade cabinets have since become collector's items with the cocktail-table version being the rarest. Soon after the game's successful testing at Andy Capp's Tavern, other companies began visiting the bar to inspect it. Similar games appeared on the market three months later, produced by companies like Ramtek and Nutting Associates. Atari could do little against the competitors

The Magnavox Odyssey, invented by Ralph H. BAER, inspired Pong's development.

as they had not initially filed for patents on the solid state technology used in the game. When the company did file for patents, complications delayed the process. As a result, the market consisted primarily of "Pong clones". Author Steven KENT estimated that Atari had produced less than a third of the machines. Bushnell referred to the competitors as "jackals" because he felt they had an unfair advantage. His solution to competing against them was to produce more innovative games and concepts.

Home Pong was an instant success following its limited 1975 release through Sears. Around 150,000 units were sold that holiday season. The game became Sears' most successful product at the time, which earned Atari a Sears Quality Excellence Award. Similar to the arcade version, several companies released clones to capitalize on the home console's success, many of which continued to produce new consoles and video games. Magnavox rereleased their Odyssey system with simplified hardware and new features, and would later release updated versions. Coleco entered the video game market with their Telstar console. It features three Pong variants and was also succeeded by newer models. Nintendo released the Color TV

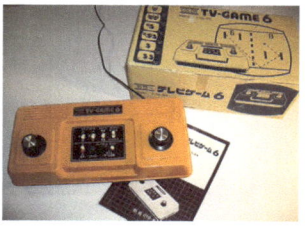

Nintendo's "Color TV Game 6".

Game 6 in 1977, which plays six variations of electronic tennis. The next year, it was followed by an updated version, the Color TV Game 15, which features fifteen variations. The systems were Nintendo's entry into the home video game market and the first to produce by themselves (they had previously licensed the Magnavox Odyssey). The dedicated Pong consoles and the numerous clones have since become varying levels of rare. Atari's Pong consoles are common, while APF Electronics' TV Fun consoles are moderately rare. Prices among collectors however, vary with rarity. The Sears Tele-Games versions are often cheaper than those with the Atari brand.

APF TV Fun Pong console. Model with two paddles in the body of the console.

Several publications consider Pong the game that launched the video game industry as a lucrative enterprise. Video game author David ELLIS sees the game as the cornerstone of the video game industry's success, and called the arcade game "one of the most historically significant" titles. Kent attributes the "arcade phenomenon" to Pong and Atari's games that followed it, and considers the release of the home version, the successful beginning of home video game consoles. Bill LOGUIDICE and Matt BARTON of Gamasutra referred to the game's release as the start of a new entertainment medium, and commented that its simple, intuitive gameplay made it a success. Many of the companies that produced their own versions of Pong eventually became well-known within the industry. Nintendo entered the video game market with clones of Home Pong.

The revenue generated from them (each system sold over a million units) helped the company survive a difficult financial time, and spurred them to pursue video games further. After seeing the success of Pong, Konami decided to break into the arcade game market and released its first title, Maze. Its moderate success drove the company to develop more titles.

## 1.6. Sequels and remakes

Bushnell felt the best way to compete against imitators was to create better products, leading Atari to produce sequels in the years following the original's release: Pong Doubles, Super Pong, Quadrapong, and Pin-Pong. The sequels feature similar graphics, but include new gameplay elements, for example, Pong Doubles allows four players to compete in pairs, while Quadrapong has them compete against each other in a four way field. Bushnell also conceptualized a free-to-play version of Pong to entertain children in a doctor's office. He initially titled it Snoopy Pong and fashioned the cabinet after Snoopy's doghouse with the character on top, but retitled it to Puppy Pong and altered Snoopy to a generic dog to avoid legal action. Bushnell later used the game in his chain of Chuck E. Cheese's restaurants. In 1976, Atari released Breakout, a single-player variation of Pong where the object of the game is to remove bricks from a wall by hitting them with a ball. Like Pong, Breakout was followed by numerous clones that copied the gameplay: Arkanoid, Alleyway, Break 'Em All.

Atari remade the game on numerous platforms. In 1977, Pong and several variants of the game were featured in Video Olympics, one of the original release titles for the Atari 2600. Pong has also been included in several Atari compilations on platforms including the Sega Mega Drive, PlayStation Portable, Nintendo DS, and personal computer. Through an agreement with Atari, Bally Gaming and Systems developed a slot machine version of the game. The Atari developed TD Overdrive includes Pong as an extra game to be played during the loading screen. In 1999, the game was remade for home computers and the PlayStation with 3D graphics and power-ups.

## 1.7. In popular culture

Pong has appeared in several facets of popular culture. The game is prominently featured in episodes of television series: That '70s Show, King of the Hill and Saturday Night Live. In 2006, an American Express commercial featured Andy RODDICK in a tennis match against the white, in-game paddle. Other video games have also referenced and parodied Pong, for example Neuromancer for the Commodore 64 and Banjo-Kazooie: Nuts and Bolts for the Xbox 360. The concert event Video Games Live has performed audio from Pong as part of a special retro "Classic Arcade Medley". Frank BLACK's song "Whatever Happened to Pong?" on the album Teenager of the Year, heavily references the game's elements.

Dutch design studio Buro Vormkrijgers created a Pong-themed clock as a fun project within their offices. After the studio decided to manufacture it for retail, Atari took legal action in February 2006. The two companies eventually reached an agreement in which Buro Vormkrijgers could produce a limited number under license.

In 1999, French artist Pierre HUYGHE created an installation entitled "Atari Light", in which, two people use handheld gaming devices to play Pong on an illuminated ceiling. The work was shown at the Venice Biennale in 2001 and the Museo de Arte Contemporáneo de Castilla y León in 2007.

The game was included in the London Barbican Art Gallery's 2002 Game On exhibition, meant to showcase the various aspects of video game history, development, and culture.

## References

http://en.wikipedia.org/wiki/Pong

http://en.wikipedia.org/w/index.php?title=Pong&action=history

https://commons.wikimedia.org/wiki/File:Atari_Pong_and_Computer_Space.jpg

http://en.wikipedia.org/wiki/File:AlAlcorn-Cropped.jpg

https://commons.wikimedia.org/wiki/File:Magnavox_Odyssey.jpg

http://en.wikipedia.org/wiki/File:TeleGames-Atari-Pong.png

https://commons.wikimedia.org/wiki/File:Al_Alcorn,_Pong,_CHM_2011.jpg

https://commons.wikimedia.org/wiki/File:Pong_paddle_-_320738380_-_axeldeviaje.jpg

https://en.wikipedia.org/wiki/File:Pong.png

http://en.wikipedia.org/wiki/File:Signed_Pong_Cabinet.jpg

https://commons.wikimedia.org/wiki/File:Atari_Video_Pinball_C-380.jpg

https://commons.wikimedia.org/wiki/File:AtariVideoPinballVer1.jpg

https://en.wikipedia.org/wiki/File:Magnavox-Odyssey-Console-Set.jpg

https://commons.wikimedia.org/wiki/File:Nintendo_tvgame_6.jpg

https://commons.wikimedia.org/wiki/File:APF_TV_Fun_(with_paddle_model).jpg

# 2. SPACE INVADERS

Space Invaders is an arcade video game developed by Tomohiro NISHIKADO and released in 1978. It was originally manufactured and sold by Taito in Japan, and was later licensed for production in the United States by the Midway division of Bally. Space Invaders is one of the earliest shooting games and the aim is to defeat waves of aliens with a laser cannon to earn as many points as possible. In designing the game, Nishikado drew inspiration from popular media: Breakout, The War of the Worlds and Star Wars. To complete it, he had to design custom hardware and development tools.

It was one of the forerunners of modern video gaming and helped expand the video game industry from a novelty to a global industry. When first released, Space Invaders was very successful.

The game has been the inspiration for other video games, rereleased on numerous platforms, and led to several sequels. The 1980 Atari 2600 version quadrupled the system's sales and became the first "killer app" for video game consoles. Space Invaders has been referenced and parodied in multiple television shows, and been a part of several video game and cultural exhibitions. The pixelated enemy alien has become a pop culture icon, often used as a synecdoche representing video games as a whole.

Space Invaders-style alien.

## 2.1. Gameplay

Space Invaders is a two-dimensional fixed shooter game in which the player controls a laser cannon by moving it horizontally across the bottom of the screen and firing at descending aliens. The aim is to defeat five rows of eleven aliens (some versions feature different numbers) that move horizontally back and forth across the screen as they advance towards the bottom of the screen. The player defeats an alien, and earns points, by shooting it with the laser cannon. As more aliens are defeated, the aliens' movement and the game's music both speed up. Defeating the aliens brings another wave that is more difficult, a loop which can continue without end.

The aliens attempt to destroy the cannon by firing at it while they approach the bottom of the screen. If they reach the bottom, the alien invasion is successful and the game ends. A special "mystery ship" will

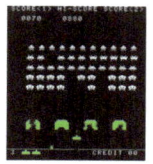

The player controlled laser cannon shoots the aliens as they descend to the bottom of the screen.

occasionally move across the top of the screen and award bonus points if destroyed. The laser cannon is partially protected by several stationary defense bunkers (the number varies by version) that are gradually destroyed by projectiles from the aliens and player.

## 2.2. Development

Space Invaders was created by Tomohiro NISHIKADO, who spent a year designing the game and developing the necessary hardware to produce it. The game's inspiration is reported to have come from varying sources, including an adaptation of the mechanical game Space Monsters released by Taito in 1972, and a dream about Japanese school children who are

A promotional flyer for Space Invaders. An arcade display on the bottom right corner is shown over a laser cannon surrounded by aliens and saucers. The background contains the screen against a background of a canyon and a block mountain. The Space Invaders and Taito logos are displayed on the top of the poster.

waiting for Santa Claus and are attacked by invading aliens. However, Nishikado has cited Atari's arcade game Breakout as his inspiration. He aimed to create a shooting game that featured the same sense of achievement from completing stages and destroying targets, but with more complex graphics. Nishikado used a similar layout to that of Breakout, but altered the game mechanics. Rather than bounce a ball to attack static objects, players are given the ability to fire projectiles at their own discretion to attack moving enemies.

Early enemy designs included tanks, combat planes, and battleships. Nishikado however, was not satisfied with the enemy movements. Technical limitations made it difficult to simulate flying. Humans would have been easier to simulate, but Nishikado considered shooting them immoral. After seeing a magazine feature about Star Wars, he thought of using a space theme. Nishikado drew inspiration for the aliens from H. G. WELLS' The War of the Worlds (he had watched the 1953 film adaptation as a child) and created initial bitmap images after the octopus-like aliens. Other alien designs were modeled after squids and crabs. The game was originally titled Space Monsters, inspired by a popular song in Japan at the time ("Monster"), but was changed to Space Invaders by Nishikado's superiors.

## 2.3. Hardware

Because microcomputers in Japan were not powerful enough at the time to perform the complex tasks involved in designing and programming Space Invaders, Nishikado had to design his own custom hardware and development tools for the game. He created the arcade board using new microprocessors from the United States. The game uses an Intel 8080 central processing unit, and features raster graphics on a CRT monitor and monaural sound hosted by a combination of analogue circuitry and a Texas

Instruments SN76477 sound chip. Despite the specially developed hardware, Nishikado was unable to program the game as he wanted (the Control Program board was not powerful enough to display the graphics in color or move the enemies faster) and he considered the development of the hardware the most difficult part of the whole process. While programming the game, Nishikado discovered that the processor was able to render the alien graphics faster, the fewer were on screen. Rather than design the game to compensate for the speed increase, he decided to keep it as a challenging gameplay mechanic.

Space Invaders was first released in a cocktail-table format with black and white graphics, while the Western release by Midway was in an upright cabinet format. The upright cabinet uses strips of orange and green cellophane over the screen to simulate color graphics. The graphics are reflected onto a painted backdrop of a moon against a starry background. Later Japanese releases also used colored cellophane. The cabinet artwork features large, humanoid monsters not present in the game. Nishikado attributes this to the artist basing the designs on the original title, Space Monsters, rather than referring to the in-game graphics.

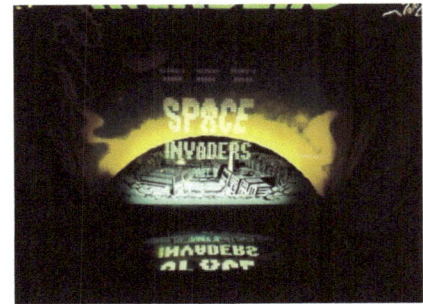

Mirrored display and cardboard background of a Midway Space Invaders Deluxe arcade cabinet.

## 2.4. Music

Despite its simplicity, the music to Space Invaders was revolutionary in the gaming industry. Videogame scholar Andrew SCHARTMANN identifies three aspects of the music that would have a significant impact on the development of game music:

1. Whereas videogame music prior to Space Invaders was restricted to the extremities (i.e., a short introductory theme with game over counterpart), the alien-inspired hit featured continuous music, the well-known four-note loop, throughout, uninterrupted by sound effects. "It was thus the first time that sound effects and music were superimposed to form a rich sonic landscape. Not only do players receive feedback related directly to their actions through sound effects, they also receive stimulus in a more subtle, noninteractive fashion through music."

2. The music interacts with on-screen animation to influence the emotions of the player. "That seemingly pedestrian four-note loop might stir us in the most primitive of ways, but that it stirs us at all is worthy of note. By demonstrating that game sound could be more than a simple tune to fill the silence, Space Invaders moved videogame music closer to the realm of art."

3. The music popularized the notion of variability, the idea that music can change in accordance with the ongoing narrative. The variable in Space Invaders (tempo) is admittedly simple, but its implications are not to be underestimated. "Over the years, analogous strategies of variation would be applied to pitch, rhythm, dynamics, form and a host of other parameters, all with the goal of accommodating the nonlinear aspect of videogames."

*"At the deepest of conceptual levels, one would be hard-pressed to find an arcade game as influential to the early history of videogame music as Space Invaders. Its role as a harbinger of the fundamental techniques that would come to shape the industry, remains more or less unchallenged. And its blockbuster success ensured the adoption of those innovations by the industry at large."*

Andrew SCHARTMANN, *Maestro Mario: How Nintendo Transformed Videogame Music into an Art*, *Thought Catalog* (2013)

## 2.5. Impact and legacy

After the first few months following its release in Japan, the game became very popular. Specialty arcades opened with nothing but Space Invaders cabinets, and by the end of 1978, Taito had installed over 100,000 machines and grossed over $600 million in Japan alone. Within two years by 1980, Taito had sold over 300,000 Space Invaders arcade machines in Japan, in addition to 60,000 machines in the

United States, where prices ranged from $2000 to $3000 for each machine, within one year. The arcade cabinets have since become collector's items with the cocktail and cabaret versions being the rarest. By mid-1981, more than four billion quarters, or $1 billion, had been grossed from Space Invaders machines, and it would continue to gross an average of $600 million a year through to 1982, by which time it had grossed $2 billion in quarters (equivalent to $4.6 billion in 2011), with a net profit of $450 million (equivalent to $1 billion in 2011). This made it the best-selling video game and highest-grossing entertainment product of its time, with comparisons made to the then highest-grossing film Star Wars, which had grossed $486 million in movie tickets (costing $2.25 each on average) with a net profit of $175 million. Space Invaders had earned Taito profits of over $500 million. The 1980 Atari 2600 version was the first official licensing of an arcade game and became the first "killer app" for video game consoles by quadrupling the system's sales. It sold

Space Invaders, cocktail or table cabinet.

over two million units in its first year on sale as a home console game, making it the first title to sell a million cartridges. Other official ports of the game were made for the Atari 8 bit computer line and Atari 5200 console. Taito released it for the NES in 1985 (Japan only). Numerous unofficial clones were made as well, such as the popular computer games Super Invader (1979) and TI Invaders (1981).

An oft-quoted urban legend states that there was a shortage of 100 yen coins, and subsequent production increase in Japan, attributed to the game, although in actuality, 100 yen coin production was lower in 1978 and 1979 than in previous or subsequent years. The claim also doesn't hold up to logical scrutiny, arcade operators would have emptied out their machines and taken the money to the bank, thus keeping the coins in circulation. Reports from those living in Japan at the time indicate "nothing out of the ordinary ... during the height of the Space Invaders invasion".

Game designer Shigeru MIYAMOTO considered Space Invaders a game that revolutionized the video game industry. He was never interested in video games before seeing it. Hideo KOJIMA also described it as the first video game that impressed him and got him interested in video games. Several publications ascribed the expansion of the video game industry from a novelty into a global industry, to the success of the game. Edge magazine attributed the shift of video games from bars and arcades to more mainstream locations like restaurants and department stores, to Space Invaders. Its popularity was such that it was the first game where an arcade machine's owner could make up for the cost of the machine in less than one month, or in some places within one week.

Technology journalist Jason WHITTAKER credited the game's success to ending the video game crash of 1977, which had earlier been caused by Pong clones flooding the market, and beginning the golden age of video arcade games. According to The Observer, the home console versions were popular and encouraged users to learn programming, many who later became industry leaders. 1UP.com stated that Space Invaders showed that video games could compete against the major entertainment media at the time: movies, music and television. IGN attributed the launch of the arcade phenomenon in North America in part to Space Invaders. Electronic Games credited the game's success as the impetus behind video gaming becoming a rapidly growing hobby and as "the single most popular coin-operated attraction of all time". Game Informer considered it, along with Pac-Man, one of the most popular arcade games that tapped into popular culture and generated excitement during the golden age of arcades. IGN listed it as one of the "Top 10 Most Influential Games" in 2007, citing the source of inspiration to video game designers and the impact it had on the shooting genre. 1UP ranked it at No. 3 in its list of "The 60 Most Influential Games of All Time", stating that, in contrast to earlier arcade games which "were attempts to simulate already existing things", Space Invaders was "the first video game as a video game, instead of merely a playable electronic representation of something else". In 2008, Guinness World Records listed it as the top-rated arcade game in technical, creative and cultural impact.

As one of the earliest shooting games, it set precedents and helped pave the way for future titles and for the shooting genre. Space Invaders popularized a more interactive style of gameplay with the enemies responding to the player controlled cannon's movement, and was the first video game to popularize the concept of achieving a high score, being the first to save the player's score. While earlier shooting games allowed the player to shoot at targets, Space Invaders was the first in which targets could fire back at the player. It was also the first game where players were given multiple lives, had to repel hordes of enemies, could take cover from enemy fire, and use destructible barriers, in addition to being the first game to use a continuous background soundtrack, with four simple diatonic descending bass notes repeating in a loop, which was dynamic and changed pace during stages, like a heartbeat sound that increases pace as enemies approached.

It also moved the gaming industry away from Pong-inspired sports games grounded in real world situations towards action games involving fantastical situations. Whittaker commented that Space Invaders helped action games become the most dominant genre on both arcades and consoles, through to contemporary times. Guinness World Records considered Space Invaders one of the most successful arcade shooting games by 2008. In describing it as a "seminal arcade classic", IGN listed it as the number eight "classic shoot 'em up". Space Invaders set the template for the shoot 'em up genre. Its worldwide success created a demand for a wide variety of science fiction games, inspiring the development of arcade games, such as Atari's Asteroids, Williams Electronics' Defender, and Namco's Galaxian and Galaga, which were modeled after Space Invaders' gameplay and design. This influence extends to most shooting games released to the present day, including first person shooters such as Wolfenstein, Doom, Halo and Call of Duty. Space Invaders also had an influence on early computer dungeon crawl games such as Dungeons of Daggorath, which used similar heartbeat sounds to indicate player health.

## 2.6. Remakes and sequels

Space Invaders has been remade on numerous platforms and spawned many sequels. Re-releases include ported and updated versions of the original arcade game. Ported versions generally feature different graphics and additional gameplay options, for example, moving defense bunkers, zigzag shots, invisible aliens, and two-player cooperative gameplay. Ports on earlier systems like the Atari home consoles featured simplified graphics, while later systems such as the Super Nintendo Entertainment System and PlayStation featured updated graphics. Later titles include several modes of gameplay and integrate new elements into the original design. For example, Space Invaders Extreme, released on the Nintendo DS and PlayStation Portable, integrated musical elements into the standard gameplay. A spin-off for WiiWare, Space Invaders Get Even, allows players to control the aliens instead of the laser cannon.

In 1980, Bally Midway released a pinball version of the game. However, few elements from the original game are included, and the aliens instead resemble the xenomorphs from the film Alien. Bally Midway was later sued over the game's resemblance to designs by H. R. GIGER. Different ports have been met with mixed receptions. The Atari 2600 version was very successful while the Nintendo Entertainment System version was poorly received.

Taito has released several arcade sequels that built upon the basic design of the original. The first was Space Invaders Part II in 1979. It featured color graphics, an attract mode, and new gameplay elements, and added an intermission between gameplay. According to the Killer List of Video Games, this was the first video game to include an intermission. The game also allowed the player with the top score to sign their name on the high score table. This version was released in the United States as Deluxe Space Invaders (also known as Space Invaders Deluxe), but featured a different graphical color scheme and a lunar city background. Another arcade sequel, titled Space Invaders II, was released exclusively in the United States. It was in a cocktail-table format with very fast alien firing and a competitive two-player mode. During the summer of 1985, Return of the Invaders was released with updated color graphics, and more complex movements and attack patterns for the aliens. Subsequent arcade sequels included Super Space Invaders '91, Space Invaders DX, and Space Invaders '95. Each game introduced minor gameplay additions to the original design. Like the original game, several of the arcade sequels have become collector's items, though some are considered rarer. In 2002, Taito released Space Raiders, a third person shooter reminiscent of Space Invaders.

The game and its related games have been included in video game compilation titles. Space Invaders Anniversary was released in 2003 for the PlayStation 2 and included nine Space Invaders variants. A similar title for the PlayStation Portable, Space Invaders Pocket, was released in 2005. Space Invaders, Space Invaders Part II and Return of the Invaders are included in Taito Legends, a compilation of Taito's classic arcade games released in 2005 on the PlayStation 2, Xbox and PC. Super Space Invaders '91, Space Invaders DX and Space Invaders '95 were included in Taito Legends 2, a sequel compilation released in 2006.

## 2.7. In popular culture

Many publications and websites use the pixelated alien graphic as an icon for video games in general, including video game magazine Electronic Gaming Monthly, technology website Ars Technica, and concert event Video Games Live. There have also been Space Invaders themed merchandising, including necklaces and puzzles.

The game, and references to it, has appeared in numerous facets of popular culture. Soon after the game's release, hundreds of favorable articles and stories about the emerging video game medium popularized by Space Invaders aired on television and were printed in newspapers and magazines. The Space Invaders Tournament held by Atari in 1980 was the first electronic sports event and attracted more than 10,000 participants, establishing video gaming as a mainstream hobby. The Arcade Awards ceremony was created that same year to honor the best video games, with Space Invaders winning the first Game of the Year award. The impact of Space Invaders on the video game industry has been compared to that of The Beatles in the pop music industry. Considered "the first blockbuster video game", Space Invaders became synonymous with video games worldwide for some time.

Within a year of the game's release, the Japanese PTA unsuccessfully attempted to ban the game for allegedly inspiring truancy. In North America, doctors identified a condition called the "Space Invaders elbow" as a complaint, while a physician in The New England Journal of Medicine named a similar ailment the "Space Invaders Wrist". Space Invaders was also the first game to attract political controversy,

A pixelated alien graphic used at the concert event Video Games Live.

when a 1981 Private Member's Bill called the "Control of Space Invaders (and other Electronic Games) Bill" drafted by British Labour Party MP George FOULKES, attempted to ban the game for its "addictive properties" and for causing "deviancy", a motion to bring the bill before Parliament was briefly debated but defeated by 114 votes to 94 votes. The bill itself was never considered by Parliament.

### 2.7.1. Music

Musicians drew inspiration for their music from Space Invaders. Video Games Live performed audio from the game as part of a special retro "Classic Arcade Medley".

The pioneering Japanese synthpop group Yellow Magic Orchestra reproduced Space Invaders sounds in its 1978 self-titled album and its hit single "Computer Game", the latter selling over 400,000 copies in the United States.

Other pop songs based on Space Invaders soon followed, including disco records such as "Disco Space Invaders" (1979) by Funny Stuff, and the hit songs "Space Invader" (1980) by The Pretenders,

"Space Invaders" (1980) by Uncle Vic and the Australian hit "Space Invaders" (1979) by Player One (known in the U. S. as Playback), which in turn provided the bassline for Jesse SAUNDERS' "On and On" (1984), the first Chicago house music track.

Space Invaders is referenced in the lyrics to Rush's 1981 hit song "Tom Sawyer", and the game is singled out for special thanks in the liner notes to the band's Permanent Waves album.

The game was also sampled in I-F's "Space Invaders Are Smoking Grass" (1997), the first electroclash record.

In honor of the game's 30th anniversary, Taito produced an album titled Space Invaders 2008. The album is published by Avex Trax and features music inspired by the game. Taito's store Taito Station also unveiled a Space Invaders themed music video.

### 2.7.2. Television

Multiple television series have aired episodes that either reference or parody the game and its elements, for example, Danger Mouse, That '70s Show, Scrubs, Chuck, Robot Chicken and The Amazing World of Gumball.

Elements are prominently featured in the "Raiders of the Lost Arcade" segment of "Anthology of Interest II", an episode of Futurama.

### 2.7.3. Other

In 2006, the game was one of several video game related media, selected to represent Japan as part of a project compiled by Japan's Agency for Cultural Affairs.

In the same year, Space Invaders was included in the London Science Museum's Game On exhibition meant to showcase the various aspects of video game history, development, and culture.

The game is also a part of the Barbican Centre's traveling Game On exhibition.

At the Belluard Bollwerk International 2006 festival in Fribourg, Switzerland, Guillaume REYMOND created a three-minute video recreation of a game of Space Invaders as part of the "Gameover" project using humans as pixels.

The GH ART exhibit at the 2008 Games Convention in Leipzig, Germany, included an art game, Invaders!, based on Space Invaders' gameplay. The creator later asked for the game to be removed from the exhibit following criticism of elements based on the September 11 attacks in the United States.

There is a bridge in Cáceres, Spain, projected by engineers Pedro PLASENCIA and Hadrián ARIAS whose pavement design is based on this game. The laser cannon, some shoots and several figures can be seen on the deck.

## References

http://en.wikipedia.org/wiki/Space_Invaders

http://en.wikipedia.org/w/index.php?title=Space_Invaders&action=history

https://commons.wikimedia.org/wiki/File:Space_invaders_alien.svg

http://en.wikipedia.org/wiki/File:SpaceInvaders-Gameplay.gif

http://en.wikipedia.org/wiki/File:Space_Invaders_flyer,_1978.jpg

http://en.wikipedia.org/wiki/File:Inv_D_playfield.jpg

https://commons.wikimedia.org/wiki/File:Space_Invaders.JPG

http://en.wikipedia.org/wiki/File:Vgltoronto.jpg

# 3. BREAKOUT

Breakout is an arcade game developed and published by Atari Inc. It was conceptualized by Nolan BUSHNELL and Steve BRISTOW, influenced by the 1972 Atari arcade game Pong, and built by Steve WOZNIAK aided by Steve JOBS. The game was ported to multiple platforms and upgraded to video games such as Super Breakout. In addition, Breakout was the basis and inspiration for books, video games, film, and the Apple II personal computer.

An early arcade flyer of Breakout.

In the game, a layer of bricks lines the top third of the screen. A ball travels across the screen, bouncing off the top and side walls of the screen. When a brick is hit, the ball bounces away and the brick is destroyed. The player loses a turn when the ball touches the bottom of the screen. To prevent this from happening, the player has a movable paddle to bounce the ball upward, keeping it in play.

Steve WOZNIAK.

## 3.1. Gameplay

Breakout begins with eight rows of bricks, with each two rows a different color. The color order from the bottom up is yellow, green, orange and red. Using a single ball, the player must knock down as many bricks as possible by using the walls and / or the paddle below, to ricochet the ball off the bricks and eliminate them. If the player's paddle misses the ball's rebound, he or she loses a turn. The player has three turns to try to clear two screens of bricks. Yellow bricks earn one point each, green bricks earn three points, orange bricks earn five points and the top-level red bricks score seven points each. The paddle shrinks to one-half its size after the ball has broken through the red row and hit the upper wall. Ball speed increases at specific intervals: after four hits, after twelve hits, and after making contact with the orange and red rows.

The maximum score achievable for one player is 896. This is done by eliminating two screens of bricks worth 448 points each. Once the second screen of bricks is destroyed, the ball in play harmlessly bounces off empty walls until the player relinquishes the game, as no additional screens are provided. However, a secret way to score beyond the 896 maximum is to play the game in two-player mode. If "Player One" completes the first screen on his or her third and last ball, then immediately and deliberately allows the ball to "drain", Player One's second screen is transferred to "Player Two" as a third screen, allowing Player Two to score a maximum of 1,344 points if he is adept enough to keep the third ball in play that long. Once the third screen is eliminated, the game is over.

## 3.2. History and development

Breakout, a discrete logic (non-microprocessor) game, was designed by Nolan BUSHNELL, Steve WOZNIAK, and Steve BRISTOW, all three who were involved with Atari and its Kee Games subsidiary. Atari produced innovative video games using the Pong hardware as a means of competition against companies making "Pong clones". Bushnell wanted to turn Pong into a single player game, where the player would use a paddle to maintain a ball that depletes a wall of bricks. Bushnell was certain the game would be popular, and the two partnered to produce a concept. Al ALCORN was assigned as the project manager, and began development with Cyan Engineering in 1975. Alcorn assigned Steve JOBS to design a prototype. Jobs was offered $750, with an award for every TTL (transistor-transistor logic) chip fewer than 50. Jobs promised to complete a prototype within four days.

Bushnell offered the bonus because he disliked how new Atari games required 150 to 170 chips. He knew that Jobs' friend Steve WOZNIAK, an employee of Hewlett-Packard, had designed a version of Pong that used about 30 chips. Jobs had little specialized knowledge of circuit board design, but knew Wozniak was capable of producing designs with a small number of chips. He convinced Wozniak to work with him, promising to split the fee evenly between them if Wozniak could minimize the number of chips. Wozniak had no sketches and instead interpreted the game from its description. To save parts, he had "tricky little designs" difficult to understand for most engineers. Near the end of development, Wozniak considered moving the high score to the screen's top, but Jobs claimed Bushnell wanted it at the bottom. Wozniak was unaware of any truth to his claims. The original deadline was met after Wozniak worked at Atari four nights straight, doing some additional designs while at his day job at Hewlett-Packard. This equated to a bonus of $5,000, which Jobs kept secret from Wozniak. Wozniak has stated he only received payment of $350. He believed for years that Atari had promised $700 for a design using fewer than 50 chips, and $1000 for fewer than 40, stating in 1984 "we only got 700 bucks for it". Wozniak was the engineer, and Jobs was the breadboarder and tester. Wozniak's original design used 42 chips, the final, working breadboard he and Jobs delivered to Atari used 44, but Wozniak said, "We were so tired we couldn't cut it down".

Atari was unable to use Wozniak's design. By designing the board with as few chips as possible, he made the design difficult to manufacture. It was too compact and complicated to be feasible with Atari's manufacturing methods. However, Wozniak claims Atari could not understand the design, and speculates "maybe some engineer there was trying to make some kind of modification to it". Atari ended up designing their own version for production, which contained about 100 TTL chips. Wozniak found the gameplay to be the same as his original creation, and could not find any differences.

The arcade cabinet uses a black and white monitor. However, the monitor has strips of colored cellophane placed over it so that the bricks appear to be in color.

## 3.3. Ports

The original arcade version of Breakout has been officially ported to several systems, such as Video Pinball, the Atari 5200 (included in Super Breakout), and the Atari 2600.

Atari 2600 home version of Breakout.

The Atari 2600 port was programmed by Brad STEWART. Stewart had been working on a backup project for the Atari 2600, which was eventually canceled. Consequently, Brad and Ian SHEPHERD were both available to program Breakout for the Atari 2600. They decided to compete in the original version of Breakout for the programming rights. In the end, Brad won. In development, he didn't receive help of the original designers (and was unaware who they were), and felt that there were few obstacles to overcome. Difficulties arose with the Television Interface Adaptor. The game was published in 1978 and was conceptually the same, but with a few key differences. First, there were only six rows of bricks. Second, the player is given five turns to clear two walls instead of three. One notable addition was the Breakthru variant, where the ball does not bounce off of the bricks, but continues through them until it hits the wall. Atari had this term trademarked and used it as a sister term to Breakout in order to describe gameplay, especially in look-alike games and remakes.

In 2010, the game was rereleased in a Taco Bell promotion, in which a series of four classic Atari game CD-ROMs (Centipede, Lunar Lander, Super Breakout and Asteroids) were given away in kids' meals, and were also available for purchase separately. Although the disc is titled Super Breakout, the game is a simulation of the original TTL Breakout, and also features an "evolved" gameplay mode. Legacy Engineering developed this series of games for the promotion.

## 3.4. Super Breakout

The success of the game resulted in the development of Super Breakout a couple of years later. While ostensibly very similar to Breakout (the layout, sound, and general behavior of the game is identical) Super Breakout is a microprocessor based game instead of discrete logic, programmed by Asteroids programmer Ed LOGG using an early M6502 chip. He developed Super Breakout after hearing that Nolan BUSHNELL, founder of Atari, wanted Breakout updated. Super Breakout can therefore be emulated in MAME and is also featured in a number of different Atari compilation packs. The original

Breakout has not been featured, since there is no processor in Breakout, the game would have been more "simulated" than emulated.

In Super Breakout, there are three different and more advanced game types from which the player can choose:

- **Double** gives the player control of two bats at the same time, one placed above the other, and two balls. Losing a life occurs only when both balls go out of play, and points are doubled while the player is able to juggle both balls without losing either.

- **Cavity** retains the single bat and ball of Breakout, but two other balls are enclosed on the other side of the wall, which the player must free before they too, can be used to destroy additional bricks. Points are increased for this, but triple points are available if the player can keep all three balls in play.

- **Progressive** also has the single bat and ball, but as the ball hits the paddle, the entire wall gradually advances downwards step by step, gaining in speed the longer the ball lasts in play.

## 3.5. Other platforms

The original iPod had an Easter egg where you could hold down the center button for a few seconds in the "About" menu, and Breakout would appear. Glu Mobile released a licensed cellular phone version of Super Breakout that includes the original game as well as updated gameplay, skins, and modes. In 2008, Atari released the game for the iPhone and iPod Touch via Apple's App Store.

The arcade and Atari 2600 versions of Super Breakout were made available on Microsoft's Game Room service for its Xbox 360 console and for Windows based PCs on May 5, 2010 and September 1, 2010 respectively.

## 3.6. Breakout 2000

There was also a reinvented Breakout 2000 game for the Atari Jaguar game console. Breakout 2000 was a 3D version of the arcade classic, designed for one or two players. The object of the game remained the same but in a 3D playfield. There were a total of ten different Phases to survive, each consisting of five playfields. Each playfield was more difficult to clear than prior one, and each Phase added even more difficulty and features.

The game featured good and bad power-ups somewhat similar to Arkanoid. There were unbreakable bricks, multi-hit bricks and stacked bricks. Ball movement was limited to the lower level of stacked bricks so breaking a lower brick would allow the stacked bricks to fall into the now vacated location. The game also featured a two-player mode that allowed two people (or a person and the computer) to compete head to head. In this mode a player's ball could loop around to the other player's playfield and break the opponent's bricks. A double "2X" bonus was awarded for breaking your opponent's bricks.

## 3.7. IBM PC and PlayStation

Breakout was once again updated for the IBM PC and also for the PlayStation. This version featured an ongoing storyline. In it, the character of Bouncer must rescue Daisy and his friends from the evil Batnix. With advice of Coach Steel, he travels to different lands to rescue his friends:

- **Tutorial:** Bouncer must break out of Batnix's prison to rescue his friends. After that, he must escape a wolf.

- **Egypt:** Against a backdrop of Egyptian desert sits a giant pyramid, its secrets hidden from view. Only total destruction will unlock all its treasures. Beneath the pyramid are secret tombs through which Bouncer must battle in order to reach the Mummy's Lair where a final battle with a mummy will rescue his first friend.

- **Farm:** Bouncer must use his Breakout skills to defeat sheep, chickens and ducks to rescue his second friend. After that, he must outrun another wolf.

- **Castle:** A giant Dragon carries a captive into a majestic, towering medieval castle surrounded by a deep moat. Bouncer must first defeat the knight guards on the drawbridge before he can enter the castle. Then Bouncer must tear down a wall and prevent the serfs from rebuilding it. Once Bouncer has completed several different challenges, he must climb the castle tower to the Dragon's nest and do battle with the Dragon to save another one of his friends.

- **Factory:** Batnix has devised an evil robot henchman to guard his captives in his diabolical factory. A series of devious, puzzle-like levels must be negotiated before Bouncer battles the deranged robot to complete his mission.

- **Space:** Bouncer launches a rocket into space in order to chase the evil Batnix and rescue Daisy. Bouncer must use his Breakout skills to deflect killer asteroids. Afterwards, he must face Batnix in a final showdown and rescue Daisy.

## 3.8. Mobile

In 2011 Atari S. A. released an updated version of Breakout, Breakout Boost. The game is similar to the original with the chief difference being the addition of improved graphics and deeper gameplay features such as power-ups (Fire, Acid, Splitting, and Grenade Balls), unique brick types (Exploding, Mystery, x4, and Metal bricks), and Boost Control. The faster your ball goes, the more points you'll get.

## 3.9. Unofficial variations

Many unofficial variations of Breakout were created for home computer platforms such as Apple II Plus, TRS-80 and PC. A version of the game called Little Brick Out was included on the DOS 3.2 System Master disk for the Apple II. Disney Club Penguin also has a version of this game called Ice Bricks in mission 3, "Case of the Missing Coins", with 10 levels.

## 3.10. Apple II

Breakout directly influenced Wozniak's design for the Apple II computer. He said, "A lot of features of the Apple II went in because I had designed Breakout for Atari. I had designed it in hardware. I wanted to write it in software now". This included his design of color graphics circuitry, the addition of game paddle support and sound, and graphics commands in Integer BASIC, with which he wrote Little Brick Out, a software clone of his own hardware game. Wozniak said in 1984:

*"Basically, all the game features were put in just so I could show off the game I was familiar with, Breakout, at the Homebrew Computer Club. It was the most satisfying day of my life [when] I demonstrated Breakout, totally written in BASIC. It seemed like a huge step to me. After designing hardware arcade games, I knew that being able to program them in BASIC was going to change the world."*

## 3.11. Pilgrim in the Microworld

Pilgrim in the Microworld is an autobiography by David SUDNOW detailing his obsession with Breakout. Sudnow describes studying the game's mechanics, visiting the manufacturer in Silicon Valley, and interviewing the programmers.

## 3.12. Super Breakout story

For Kid Stuff Records, John BRADEN recorded a 7-in 33$^{1/3}$ RPM record telling the story of Super Breakout. This science fiction story dealt with NASA astronaut Captain John Stewart CHANG returning from a routine mission transporting titanium ore from Io to space station New California. He encounters a rainbow barrier, presumably a force of nature that seems to have no end on either side. He has three lobbing missiles of white light that he can bounce off the hull of his shuttle, and they prove able to break through the layers of the force field. With his life support systems failing, what follows is a test of endurance turned game as he strives to break through the barrier in space.

## 3.13. Other games

Since the original release of Breakout, there have been many clones and updates for various platforms, known as "Breakout clones".

- Arcade remakes include Atari's own Super Breakout and Taito's Arkanoid as well as Namco's Quester.

- Handheld devices have had variants included with them as well. The most notable are those designed for rotary control, such as the iPod and the BlackBerry's Brick Breaker. The iriver got Brickmania on the RockBox OS. An earlier handheld variant was Nintendo's Alleyway, released in 1989 for the original Game Boy system.

- Microvision, the earliest handheld device with swappable cartridges, ca 1979, shipped with Block Buster, a simplistic Breakout clone.

- The bonus stage in Pinball plays like Breakout.

- An updated version called Bebop was made in the 1990s.

- A mini game in Major Havoc, was played for a few seconds before starting each level.

- Later versions of Turbo Pascal included Breakout, with source code, as an example of the Object Pascal language.

- A mini game in Sonic the Hedgehog (2006), is based on Breakout.

- Peggle is based on a combination of pachinko machines along with the mechanics of Breakout.

- Hardball is a free computer game similar to Breakout which was made for the Palm OS.

- A BASIC version of Breakout called "Thro' the wall" was included as part of the Horizons welcome and introduction package for the ZX Spectrum computer.

- The Miniclip puzzle game "Smashing".

## 3.14. Film

Breakout is shown in the movie Jobs.

The sci-fi short film Against the Wall directed by David CAPURSO and starring Russ RUSSO, was inspired by the Breakout style of video game.

## 3.15. Google commemorative version

On the 37th anniversary of the game's release, Google released a secret version of Breakout. In order for users to access it, they had to type "Atari Breakout" on the Images search section. After clicking enter, the search makes the images turn different colors and a little ball and stick are seen at the bottom. This is still accessible as of the release date.

## References

http://en.wikipedia.org/wiki/Breakout_(video_game)

http://en.wikipedia.org/w/index.php?title=Breakout_(video_game)&action=history

http://en.wikipedia.org/wiki/File:BreakOut_arcadeflyer.png

http://en.wikipedia.org/wiki/File:Steve_Wozniak.jpg

http://en.wikipedia.org/wiki/File:Breakout2600.png

## 4. LUNAR LANDER

A decade had passed since humans set foot on the moon, when Atari decided to give their quarter-bearing customers a whack at it. Released in 1979, Lunar Lander was a challenging, pressure-filled adventure that probably sucked up enough quarters during its short existence to finance the real Apollo mission.

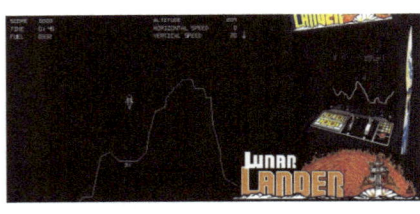

Lunar Lander.

Lunar Lander's screen displayed simple vector graphics of the Moon's surface that turned out to be surprisingly rocky and jagged. Those hoping for a soft landing on a landscape of green cheese, were in for a rude surprise. The lander had thrusters to counteract gravity and could rotate clockwise or counterclockwise. Points were awarded for successful landings, proportionate to the difficulty of the terrain. A throttle controlled thruster burn, two buttons rotated the lander in either direction, and a third 'abort' button was your last chance in case something went wrong.

The game offered several levels of difficulty that featured increasingly harder landing surfaces. From Training to Cadet to Prime to Command, players of all skill levels could try their luck at bringing down the lander. The screen displayed a wealth of information based on real world physics, like altitude, horizontal and vertical speed and fuel levels. Approach and landing used up fuel and if your lander was still in the air when that fuel ran out, it was a fast, short fall to the surface. Thankfully, pumping more quarters into the game bought you more fuel.

Lunar Lander remained a popular arcade game until Atari unleashed another space-based vector graphics game later that year, called Asteroids. It's safe to say we all know who won that war. Still, Lunar Lander lives on in the hearts of many as one of their earliest arcade game memories. And if you really get a hankering' to play, it's pretty easy to find online versions.

### References

http://www.retroland.com/lunar-lander/

# 5. ASTEROIDS

Asteroids is an arcade space shooter released in November 1979 by Atari Inc. and designed by Lyle RAINS and Ed LOGG. The player controls a spaceship in an asteroid field which is periodically traversed by flying saucers. The object of the game is to shoot and destroy asteroids and saucers while not colliding with either, or being hit by the saucers' counter fire. The game becomes harder as the number of asteroids increases.

Asteroids was conceived during a meeting between Logg and Rains and used hardware developed by Howard DELMAN previously used for Lunar Lander. Based on an unfinished game titled Cosmos and inspired by Spacewar! and Computer Space, both early shoot 'em up video games, Asteroids' physics model and control scheme were derived by Logg from these earlier games and refined through trial and error. The game is rendered on a vector display in a two-dimensional view that wraps around in both screen axes.

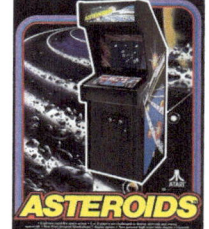

Acclaimed by players and video game critics for its vector graphics, controls and addictive gameplay, Asteroids was one of the first major hits of the golden age of arcade games. The game sold over 70,000 arcade cabinets and proved both popular with players and influential with developers. It has since been ported to multiple platforms. Asteroids was widely imitated and directly influenced two popular and often cloned arcade games, Defender and Gravitar, as well as many other video games.

A promotional flyer for Asteroids, featuring the arcade cabinet over a background of floating asteroids surrounding a planet. The Asteroids logo and details about the game are seen in the bottom of the flyer.

## 5.1. Gameplay

The objective of Asteroids is to destroy asteroids and saucers. The player controls a triangular ship that can rotate left and right, fire shots straight forward, and thrust forward. Once the ship begins moving in a direction, it will continue in that direction for a time without player intervention unless the player applies thrust in a different direction. The ship eventually comes to a stop when not thrusting. The player can also send the ship into hyperspace, causing it to disappear and reappear in a random location on the screen, at the risk of self-destructing or appearing on top of an asteroid.

Each level starts with a few large asteroids drifting in various directions on the screen. Objects wrap around screen edges, for instance, an asteroid that drifts off the top edge of the screen reappears at the bottom and continues moving in the same direction. As the player shoots asteroids, they break into smaller asteroids that move faster and are more difficult to hit. Smaller asteroids are also worth more points. Two flying saucers appear periodically on the screen, the "big saucer" shoots randomly and poorly, while the "small saucer" fires frequently at the ship. After reaching a score of 40,000, only the small saucer appears. As the player's score increases, the angle range of the shots from the small saucer diminishes until the saucer fires extremely accurately. Once the screen has been cleared of all asteroids and flying saucers, a new set of large asteroids appears, thus starting the next level. The game gets harder as the number of asteroids increases until after the score reaches a range between 40,000 and 60,000. The player starts with 3 lives after a coin is inserted and gains an extra life every 10,000 points. When the player loses all his lives, the game ends.

Ed LOGG standing next to a very rare "Gold Asteroids" cabinet at Atari. Photo taken Spring 1999 at Atari Games in Milpitas, California.

Like many games of its time, Asteroids contains several bugs. The game slows down as the player gains 50-100 lives, due to a programming error in that there is no limit for the permitted number of lives. The player can "lose" the game after more than 250 lives are collected.

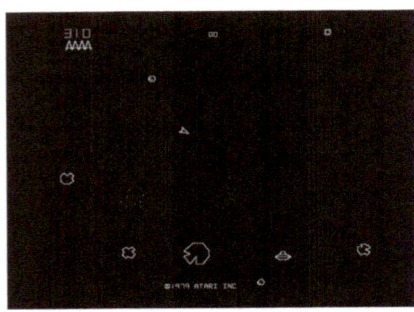

A ship is surrounded by asteroids and a saucer.

## 5.2. Development and design

Asteroids was conceived by Lyle RAINS and programmed by Ed LOGG with collaborations from other Atari staff. Logg was impressed with the Atari 2600 (then known as "Atari Video Computer System") and joined Atari's coin-op division and worked on Dirt Bike, which was never released due to an unsuccessful field test. He developed Super Breakout after hearing that Nolan BUSHNELL, founder of Atari, wanted Breakout updated. Paul MANCUSO joined the development team as Asteroids' technician and engineer Howard DELMAN contributed to the hardware. During a meeting in April 1979, Rains discussed Planet Grab, a multiplayer arcade game later renamed to Cosmos. Logg did not know the name of the game, thinking Computer Space as "the inspiration for the two-dimensional approach". The unfinished game featured a giant, indestructible asteroid, so Rains asked Logg: "Well, why don't we have a game where you shoot the rocks and blow them up?" In response, Logg described a similar concept where the player selectively shoots at rocks that break into smaller pieces. Both agreed on the concept.

Asteroids was implemented on hardware developed by Delman and is a vector game, in which the graphics are composed of lines drawn on a vector monitor. Rains initially wanted the game done in raster graphics, but Logg, experienced in vector graphics, suggested an XY monitor because the high 1024 x 760 resolution would permit precise aiming. The hardware is chiefly a MOS 6502 executing the game program, and QuadraScan, a high-resolution vector graphics processor developed by Atari and referred to as an "XY display system" and the "Digital Vector Generator (DVG)".

The original design concepts for QuadraScan came out of Cyan Engineering, Atari's off-campus research lab in Grass Valley, California, in 1978. Cyan gave it to Delman, who finished the design and first used it for Lunar Lander. Logg received Delman's modified board with five buttons, 13 sound effects, and additional RAM, and used it to develop Asteroids. The size of the board was 4 by 4 inches, and it was "linked up" to a monitor.

Logg modeled the player's ship, the five-button control scheme, and the game physics after Spacewar!, which he had played as a student at the University of California, Berkeley, but made several changes to improve playability. The ship was programmed into the hardware and rendered by the monitor, and was configured to move with thrust and inertia. The hyperspace button was not placed near Logg's right thumb, which he was dissatisfied, as he had a problem "tak[ing] his hand off the thrust button". Drawings of asteroids in various shapes were incorporated into the game. Logg copied the idea of a high score table with initials from Exidy's Star Fire.

The two saucers were formulated to be different from each other. A steadily decreasing timer that shortens intervals between saucer attacks was employed to keep the player from not shooting asteroids and saucers. The minimalist soundtrack features a "heartbeat" sound effect, which quickens as the game progresses. The game did not have a sound chip, so Delman created a hardware circuit for 13 sound effects by hand which was wired onto the board.

Shape of big asteroid of arcade game Asteroids, simple geometry.

A prototype of Asteroids was well received by several Atari staff and engineers, who would "wander between labs, passing comment and stopping to play as they went". Logg was often asked when he would be leaving by employees eager to play the prototype, so he created a second prototype specifically for staff to play. Atari went to Sacramento, California for testing, setting up prototypes of the game in local arcades to measure its potential success. The company also observed veteran players and younger players during focus group sessions at Atari itself. A group of old players familiar with Spacewar! struggled to maintain grip on the thrust button and requested a joystick, whereas younger players accustomed to Space Invaders noted they get no break in the game. Logg and other Atari engineers observed proceedings and documented comments in four pages.

## 5.3. Reception and legacy

Asteroids was immediately successful upon release. It displaced Space Invaders by popularity in the United States and became Atari's best-selling arcade game of all time, with over 70,000 units sold. Atari earned an estimated $150 million in sales from the game, and arcade operators earned further $500 million from coin drops. Atari had been in the process of manufacturing another vector game, Lunar Lander, but demand for Asteroids was so high "that several hundred Asteroids games were shipped in

Lunar Lander cabinets". Asteroids was so popular that some video arcade operators had to install large boxes to hold the number of coins spent by players.

The saucer in the original game design was supposed to take a shot as soon as it appeared. This action was altered so there would be a delay before the saucer shoots, leading to "lurking" from players. Lurking is a strategy in which the player uses thrust to keep the ship in motion, leaves 1 or 2 asteroids undamaged, and hunts for saucers, allowing the player to pick off as many 1,000-point UFOs as possible and play indefinitely on a single credit. Since the saucer could only shoot directly at the player's position on the screen, the player could "hide" at the opposite end of the screen and shoot across the screen boundary, while remaining relatively safe. Complaints from operators losing revenue due to lurking, led to the creation of an EPROM restricting such chances. Usage of the names of Saturday Night Live characters "Mr. Bill" and "Sluggo" to refer to the saucers in an Esquire article about the game, led to Logg receiving a cease and desist letter from a lawyer with the "Mr. Bill Trademark".

Asteroids received positive reviews from video game critics and has been regarded as Logg's magnum opus. Brett Alan WEISS, writing for Allgame, likened the monochrome vector graphics to minimalism and viewed its sound effects as memorable. Weiss found its overall design to be near perfect and cites the intensity and controls as elements that make the game addicting. He admitted the game is easily understandable and "holds up extremely well over time". William CASSIDY, writing for GameSpy's "Classic Gaming", noticed its innovations, including being one of the first video games to track initials and allow players to enter their initials for appearing in the top 10 high scores, and commented, "the vector graphics fit the futuristic outer space theme very well". Asteroids was ranked fourth on Retro Gamer's list of "Top 25 Arcade Games". The Retro Gamer staff cited its simplicity and the lack of a proper ending as allowances of revisiting the game. It was added to the Museum of Modern Art's collection of video games.

Released in 1981, Asteroids Deluxe is the first sequel to Asteroids. Dave SHEPPERD edited the code and made enhancements to the game without Logg's involvement. The onscreen objects were tinted blue, and hyperspace was replaced by a shield that depleted if used. The asteroids rotate, and the added killer satellite enemy breaks apart into three smaller ships when hit that home the player's position. The arcade machine's monitor displays vector graphics overlaying a holographic backdrop. It was followed by Owen RUBIN's Space Duel in 1982, featuring colorful geometric shapes and co-op multiplayer gameplay, and Blasteroids in 1987, in which Ed ROTBERG added "power-ups, ship morphing, branching levels, bosses and the ability to dock your ships in multiplayer for added firepower". Asteroids: Gunner, released to iOS platforms in 2011, has a large amount of content as a free to play game, with 150 waves, power-ups, and an achievement system.

The gameplay in Asteroids was imitated by many games that followed, mostly "Asteroid clones". The Mattel Intellivision title Astrosmash was conceived as Avalanche! after Meteor! did not take up the cartridge's entire ROM space. Meteor!, an Asteroids clone, was cancelled to avoid a lawsuit and

Avalanche! was released as Astrosmash. The resultant game borrows elements from Asteroids and Space Invaders, as with Defender and Gravitar, two popular and often cloned arcade games.

Quality Software's Asteroids in Space (1980), another Asteroids clone, was one of the best-selling games for the Apple II and was voted one of the most popular software titles of 1978 - 80 by Softalk magazine. Others include Acornsoft's Meteors and Ambrosia Software's Maelstrom, as well as those with expanded gameplay and background, such as Moons of Jupiter for the Commodore VIC-20 and MineStorm for the Vectrex.

In 2009, Universal Studios won the rights to adapt Asteroids into a film, with Matthew LOPEZ as the scriptwriter and Lorenzo di BONAVENTURA as the producer. The game has no plot, so Universal would create the story from scratch, as done with Battleship, a film based on the Hasbro board game of the same name.


## 5.4. Ports

Asteroids has been ported to multiple platforms, including much of Atari's hardware (Atari 2600 in 1981, Atari 7800 in 1986, Atari Lynx in 1994) and many other platforms. Released in 1981, the 2600 port was the first game to use bank switching, a technique developed by Carl NIELSEN's group of engineers that increased available ROM space from 4 KB to 8 KB. Brad STEWART, the programmer tasked to work on the port, used bank switching to complete the game. A port was in development for the Atari 5200 but was never officially released. The Atari 7800 version is a launch title and features cooperative play. The asteroids receive colorful textures, and the "heartbeat" sound effect remains intact. The game was included as part of the Atari Lynx title Super Asteroids & Missile Command, and featured in the original Microsoft Arcade compilation in 1993, the latter with four other Atari video games: Missile Command, Tempest, Centipede and Battlezone.

Activision made an enhanced version of Asteroids for PlayStation, Nintendo 64, Microsoft Windows and the Game Boy Color in 1998. Doug PERRY, writing for entertainment and video game journalism website IGN, praised the high-end graphics, with realistic space object models, backgrounds, and special effects, for making Asteroids "a pleasure to look at" while being a homage to the original arcade version. The Atari Flashback series of dedicated video game consoles have included both the 2600 and the arcade versions of Asteroids.

Published by Crave Entertainment on December 14, 1999, Asteroids Hyper 64 is the Nintendo 64 port of Asteroids. The game's graphics were upgraded to 3D, with both the ship and asteroids receiving polygon models along static backgrounds, and it was supplemented with weapons and a multiplayer mode. IGN writer Matt CASAMASSINA was pleased that the gameplay was faithful to the original but felt the minor additions and constant "repetition" was not enough to make the port "warrant a $50 purchase". He was disappointed about the lack of music and found the sound effects to be of poor quality.

In 2001, Infogrames released Atari Anniversary Edition for the Sega Dreamcast, PlayStation and PC compatibles. Developed by Digital Eclipse, it included emulated versions of Asteroids and other old Atari games. Jeff GERSTMANN of Gamespot criticized the Dreamcast version for its limitations, such as the presentation of vector graphics on a low resolution television set, which obscures the copyright text in Asteroids. The arcade and Atari 2600 versions of Asteroids, along with Asteroids Deluxe, were included in Atari Anthology for both Xbox and PlayStation 2.

**A ship fires at one of the glowing asteroids. The Xbox Live Arcade port of Asteroids includes revamped HD graphics.**

Released on November 28, 2007, the Xbox Live Arcade port of Asteroids has revamped HD graphics along with an added intense "throttle monkey" mode. Both Asteroids in its arcade and 2600 versions and Asteroids Deluxe were ported to Microsoft's Game Room download service in 2010. Glu Mobile released a mobile phone port of the game with supplementary features as well as the original arcade version.

Asteroids was included on Atari Greatest Hits Volume 1 for the Nintendo DS. Craig HARRIS, writing for IGN, noticed that the Nintendo DS's small screen cannot properly display details of games with vector graphics.

## 5.5. Highest score

On November 13, 1982, 15 year old Scott SAFRAN of Cherry Hill, New Jersey, set a world record of 41,336,440 points on the arcade game Asteroids, beating the 40,101,910 point score set by Leo DANIELS of Carolina Beach on February 6, 1982. In 1998, to congratulate Safran on his accomplishment, the Twin Galaxies Intergalactic Scoreboard searched for him for four years until 2002, when it was discovered that he had died in an accident in 1989. In a ceremony in Philadelphia on April 27, 2002, Walter DAY of Twin Galaxies presented an award to the surviving members of Safran's family, commemorating the Asteroid Champion's achievement. On April 6, 2010, John McALLISTER broke Safran's record with a high score of 41,338,740 in a 58-hour Internet live stream.

## References

http://en.wikipedia.org/wiki/Asteroids_(video_game)

http://en.wikipedia.org/w/index.php?title=Asteroids_(video_game)&action=history

http://en.wikipedia.org/wiki/File:Asteroids-arcadegame.jpg

https://commons.wikimedia.org/wiki/File:Ed_Logg.jpg

http://en.wikipedia.org/wiki/File:Asteroi1.png

https://commons.wikimedia.org/wiki/File:Shape_asteroid_of_asteroids_arcade_game.png

http://en.wikipedia.org/wiki/File:Asteroids_360.jpg

# 6. SUPERMAN

Superman is an Atari 2600 game designed by John DUNN and published by Atari Inc. in 1979.

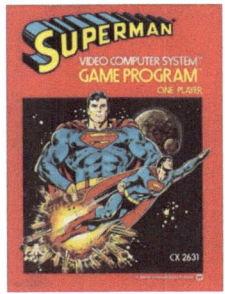

**Cover art.**

## 6.1. Gameplay

The player(s) takes control of the DC Comics character Superman, who must repair the bridge destroyed by Lex LUTHOR, capture Luthor and his criminal underlings, enter a phone booth to turn back into Clark KENT, then return to the Daily Planet in the shortest amount of time. To slow Superman's progress, kryptonite has been released by Luthor. If hit by kryptonite, Superman loses his abilities to capture criminals and fly. To regain them, he must find and kiss Lois LANE.

Three of Superman's powers are used in this game: strength, X-ray vision, and flight.

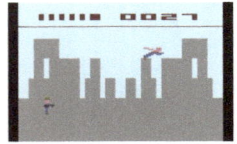

**1979 "Superman" video game.**

The game can be played with two players. The player using the left joystick controller will have priority over the left and right movement of Superman, while the player using the right controller will have priority over up and down movement of Superman.

Superman is one of the earliest console games to feature a Pause option which could be activated by pressing the select switch on the Atari 2600. The pause feature does have a bug that allows the game to be completed without having to repair the bridge or capture Lex and his gang.

### References

http://en.wikipedia.org/wiki/Superman_(1979_video_game)

http://en.wikipedia.org/w/index.php?title=Superman_(1979_video_game)&action=history

http://en.wikipedia.org/wiki/File:Superman-Atari-2600.jpg

http://en.wikipedia.org/wiki/File:Superman_Atari_2600_screenshot1a.png

www.ingramcontent.com/pod-product-compliance
Lightning Source LLC
Chambersburg PA
CBHW050837180526
45159CB00004B/1942